Michigan Publishing

Manufactured in the United States of America

This book was created for the course titled "Nature, Culture, & Landscape" taught by Sara Adlerstein at the University of Michigan, School for Environment & Sustainability. The objective was to create a book that uses the topic of urban gardening to teach young readers about the importance of environmental stewardship— respecting and caring for Earth and the diversity of life it sustains.

This book is dedicated to migratory birds of all species, whose courage and perseverance along their long journeys is an inspiration to many of us.

And to thoughtful humans who seek out ways to help them in this world we all share.

The summer days passed by full of green and the tart red of wild raspberries. The sun sparkled off the Great Lake illuminating the clear blues and purples of the deep, fresh water.

In the forest, porcupines lumbered their way through the underbrush and the white-tailed deer traced their thin paths along the ridge.

Near the shore, where the breeze from the lake stirs the whispering aspen leaves, lived a young robin. Born in the late spring, the robin had only known the beauty and warmth of summer. However, he had lately begun to feel restless.

Now, the days were shorter and the breeze off the lake blew sharp and cold.

The green leaves of summer had started to change into the ember hues of autumn.

One day, when the leaves began to fall, the young robin knew it was time to leave.

So, following his flock south, he spread his wings and took to the graying sky.

He had never seen the world from this height. The land rolled away toward the horizon in bright swathes of golden yellow, burnt orange, and red like the new, rusty color of his breast. Flying over his forest home, he could see farms and orchards cut like rectangular patches from the landscape below.

Every so often in their journey, the flock would descend to find food and rest before continuing south.

The land quickly became unfamiliar to the young robin. Forest turned to farmland, which became crossed with thick gray bands of road, cars zipping along like lines of tiny ants. Soon these roads covered the whole landscape, all leading to a central colony of opaque smoke and shining metal.

When nighttime came, this new land shone as bright as the sun but blinding and cold. The young robin no longer knew where he was or where he was going.

As the flock made their descent, large buildings of glass suddenly appeared behind the light, almost knocking them out of the air.

Once within the city, the robin's ears were filled with overpowering noise. He searched for the familiar fields and forests of his home where he could find fruit and berries to fuel his long flight. But here, there was nothing but tall pillars of brick and stone.

Eventually taking shelter in a tangle of brittle honeysuckle, the young robin fell into a fitful sleep awakened by his hunger and the shrill honks of car horns.

When morning came, the flock finally left the city, moving once more through patches of farmland.

This land was vast.

There were no forests below. Empty fields stretched as far as the eye could see, accented by occasional grain elevators and silos, the concrete columns of coal plants and smoke, and the distant rumble of freight trains.

The flock kept flying south over this flat, uniform land, stopping every so often to pick at what scarce food could be found.

After several long days, the young robin once again saw the land turn hard and gray. He saw buildings stretching tall into the sky and bright lights that blinded him.

The robin was hungry and tired. He remembered the cold, lifeless place he had passed through before and his spirits fell. He wished he were back in the forests of his home. He did not know how to find comfort here after travelling so far.

The young robin was beginning to lose hope when, to his amazement, the flock landed in a shrub filled with ripe berries!

They had arrived in a lush, green garden covered in plants with delicious fruit and seeds. There was even a small pool of fresh, running water. They couldn't be in the city, the young robin thought. But just outside the walls of the garden he could hear the telltale honks, beeps, and rush of urban living.

As the robin ate his fill of berries, he noticed that he and his flock were not alone. Many other species of birds were resting and refueling for their own southern migrations. Butterflies landing on surrounding flowers slowly opened and closed their papery wings. The robin could see the bumpy top of a frog's head glistening barely above the surface of the pool.

Sheltered by the garden, the young robin fell into a deep and peaceful sleep.

The robin awoke the next morning feeling rested. He thanked the garden for the strength it gave him to continue his journey.

The robin and his flock once again took to the skies for the last part of their migration.

Once in the air, the robin was happy to see more of these gardens spread throughout the town. He had found comfort and rest here. This time, the robin left the city feeling hopeful.

As he continued to fly over land bearing the scars of human industry, the robin kept these gardens in mind as examples of how humans have welcomed nature back to their homes.

The robin thought about all he had seen on his flight. He had learned about all the different places connected across the land. Throughout his travels, he saw forest turn into farmland, farmland into cities, and cities into gardens.

Until finally, after a long journey, the young robin and his flock arrived in the lush woodlands of their winter home.

About the Robin

In addition to being the state bird of Michigan, the American Robin is commonly known in the United States to be the harbinger of spring. This is because male robins begin singing as soon as they reach their breeding territory in March, right at the beginning of spring. In the winter, most robins leave their spring and summer range and migrate south to warmer states like Florida or even all the way to Guatemala! Robins are special in that they can migrate both during the day and at night. Many songbirds only migrate at night in order to avoid predators and use the stars to navigate. American Robins usually migrate during the day in the fall and at night in the spring. Though most robins migrate, some do not and will stay in their northern habitats through the winter. Robins migrate in response to lack of food abundance rather than colder temperatures. It is therefore important to include plants in your garden that produce fruit late into the fall so that migratory birds can find food and shelter on their journeys.

Urban Gardens

Creating urban gardens is a very rewarding way to help wildlife in your own backyard. Not only do these gardens provide food and habitat for birds but they also shelter frogs and toads, chipmunks, butterflies, and a variety of other animals. Gardens are a relaxing space for humans as well. Plus, urban gardens are often more cost-effective than simple grass lawns. Here's how you can start turning your yard into a beautiful urban garden:

- The first, and most important, aspect of growing a garden for local wildlife is to fill your garden with native plants. These are the plants that wildlife already know and love!
- Browse local plant lists and choose a variety of plants with different functions. If you want to provide food for specific birds, look up what plants they like to eat. Robins, for example, love fruiting plants such as mulberries or blackberry bushes.
- Make sure you include a water source for wildlife. This can be a small pond, fountain, or bird bath. This will also bring a greater diversity of animals to your yard including frogs and toads!
- Look at plants in the wild for inspiration! Volunteer with plant rescues and reseeding efforts to gain familiarity with your native plants. Look at plants in local gardens to see what care those plants may need in such specialized conditions.
- And, last but not least, plant what makes you happy! Not only do urban gardens enrich the lives of wildlife but they will also be a source of joy for you.

The Robin's Journey In Review

The Great Lakes

The Great Lakes form the largest fresh-water system in the world. The robin in this story lives along the shore of Lake Michigan, in Michigan's lower peninsula.

Along the lakeshore there are many smaller lakes. This image depicts Glen Lakes, near Sleeping Bear National Lakeshore. The ecosystem includes stands of hardwood forests, dunes, streams, wetlands, and the geologic remnants of glacial activity

The Midwest

Midwestern cities like Chicago can pose problems for migratory birds like the robin in this story. The bright lights can disorient flocks of traveling birds, who can get lost and may crash into buildings by accident. It is very important that food sources, like the berries and seeds in thoughtful gardens, are available for these winged travelers.

The American Midwest is largely devoted to agriculture, or farming. In particular, large fields of the same crops, called monocultures, cover the land for miles and miles. Without local plants and forests, animals have a difficult time finding food to eat and habitat to live in.

The South and the Gulf Coast

Like the large cities of the Midwest, migratory birds face similar difficulties in southern cities like New Orleans, Houston, and Dallas, which fall along their migratory path.

Urban gardens made by families and communities can make cities much less dangerous for birds like the robin in this story.

Robins and other birds fly along the Gulf Coast to reach their winter homes, where they can be warm and well fed until it becomes warm enough for them to fly north!